NANJING

南 京

FOREIGN LANGUAGES PRESS   BEIJING

外文出版社　北京

NANJING

Nanjing is a famous historic city described as "a birthplace of southern beauties and a habitat of royal rulers" by ancient Chinese poets. Historically known as Jinling, Jianye, Jiankang, Jiangning or Tianjing, Nanjing ranks with Xi'an, Luoyang, Beijing, Hangzhou and Kaifeng as six major ancient Chinese capitals.

The fossils of Homo sapiens and those of ape-men's skull caps discovered at Tangshan in the east suburbs of Nanjing indicate that Nanjing was home to a large community of human beings in the late period of the mid-Pleistocene epoch 350,000 years ago. As far back as the late Spring and Autumn Period (770-475 B.C.) Prince Fu Chai of the state of Wu erected a "metallurgical city" in the vicinity of present-day Chaotiangong, where large quantities of bronze vessels were cast and smelt. After the conquest of Wu by the state of Yue in 472 B.C., under the supervision of Minister Fan Li a "Yue city" was built at Changganli outside today's Zhonghua Gate. This event, which took place almost 2,470 years ago, resulted in the emergence of a walled city at Nanjing.

In A.D. 229 Emperor Sun Quan of the Wu Kingdom in the Three Kingdoms Period made Nanjing (known as Jianye at the time) his capital, which had its central axis at today's Taiping Road, with the Qinhuai River in the south and Xuanwu Lake in the north, and was crisscrossed by bustling streets. After that, Nanjing was again made national capital (then known as Jiankang) of Eastern Jin (317-420) and of Song, Qi, Liang and Chen in the Southern Dynasties Period (420-589), thereby earning for the city its fame as the "ancient capital of six dynasties." Nanjing in those periods boasted a brilliant culture, a thriving commerce, and a large population of anything up to 1,400,000 people. Promotion of Buddhism by emperors of successive periods brought about in Nanjing an ecclesiastical population of well over 100,000 monks and nuns and a host of magnificent temples and monasteries. "Four hundred and eighty temples from the Southern Dynasties remain standing imposingly there / Glittering towers and pavilions please the eye in the mist and rain," to quote from a poem by the celebrated Tang Dynasty poet Du Mu.

In the Five Dynasties Period following Sui and Tang, when the rest of China was torn by wars among various states contending for supremacy the Southern Tang Dynasty with its capital at Jinling was still able to exercise sovereignty in that part of China south of the Yangtze River. It witnessed no notable wars for upwards of 70 years, during which period the marketplaces and bazaars on both banks of the Qinhuai River thronged with businessmen from far and near. The prospering of the economy brought in its wake a flourishing culture and the emergence of a galaxy of outstanding poets, painters and calligraphers.

Nanjing became the nation's political center again in 1368, when Zhu Yuanzhang (r.1368-1398) founded the Ming Dynasty and named the city his capital. It took him 21 years to build a wall 33.65 kilometers in girth around Nanjing, then the largest city in the world.

In 1853, when the Taiping peasant insurgents stormed into Nanjing they made it the capital of their Taiping Heavenly Kingdom and renamed it Tianjing (Heavenly Capital), a name which stayed for only 11 years. Dr. Sun Yat-sen established the Republic of China and was chosen as its Provisional President in Nanjing on December 29, 1911, after the victory of the 1911 Revolution that ended the monarchy of the Qing Dynasty. Nanjing became the capital of the Republic on April 18, 1927, when Chiang Kai-shek proclaimed the inauguration of his National Government there.

Nanjing has undulating hills and mountains on all four sides, with the towering Purple Mountain in the east; the craggy Mufu Hill in the north; the crouching tiger-like Qingliang (Cool and Refreshing) Hill in the west, where the area around the Qingliang Temple and Saoye Tower on the slope is said to be the site of a summer resort of Li Yu (961-975), the last emperor of the Southern Tang Dynasty; the Rain Flower Terrace (Yuhuatai) in the south, renowned for its colorful pebbles; the Niushou (Ox Head) Hill, the birthplace of the Niutou (OX Pate) Sect of Chinese Buddhism, and the Zutang Hill, site of the mausoleums of the first and second Southern Tang emperors Li Bian (937-943) and Li Jing (943- 961); the Xixia (Cloud Nestling) Hill in the northeast, which is crimsoned through by its serried red maple and oak woods deep-dyed in the depth of autumn; and the Swallow Cliff (Yanziji) precipitously overlooking the Yangtze River like a swallow about to take flight.

Apart from hills and mountains, Nanjing has many rivers and lakes, such as the Qinhuai, Jinchuan, Xuanwu and Mochou, as well as the Yangtze. No wonder that while speaking of Nanjing Zhuge Liang, prime minister of the Shu Kingdom in the Three Kingdoms Period, should exclaim, ``This is indeed an abode of kings and emperors, with the Zhongshan Mountain like a curling dragon and the Stone City like a crouching tiger!''

Nanjing takes pride in an abundance of places of scenic or historical interest created by its environment, culture and celebrities: the magnificent Emperor Sun Quan, Emperor Zhu Yuanzhang and Dr. Sun Yat-sen mausoleums at the foothill of the Purple Mountain in the east suburbs; the Beamless Hall in Linggu (Soul Valley) Temple, the Monument to Martyrs of the Northern Expeditionery Force of the National Revolutionary Army, and the Sun Yat-sen Classics Depositary; and the stone sculptures in the Southern Dynasties Period's tombs. The Zhan (Prospect) and Xu (Radiance) gardens downtown are two gems of southern garden-landscaping art of the Ming and Qing dynasties. The Zhonghua Gate castle and the Ming Dynasty city wall, both the largest extant in China, and the famed Nanjing Yangtze River Bridge are also tourist destinations.

Present-day Nanjing, capital of Jiangsu Province, ranks fifth among the "50 strongest" of Chinese cities. It is a transport and telecommunication hub in East China, and the second largest international trade port after Shanghai in the Yangtze River Delta.

南　京

"江南佳丽地，金陵帝王州"。

南京是中国著名的历史文化名城，与西安、洛阳、北京、杭州、开封并称为中国的六大古都。先后称金陵、建业、建康、江宁、天京等。

在南京东郊汤山发现的古人类化石遗址和猿人头骨化石，标志着早在 35 万年前的中更新世晚期，南京就是人类的聚居之地。春秋（公元前 770 －前 475 年）末年吴王夫差就已经在今朝天宫一带筑冶城，冶铸铜器。公元前 472 年，越国灭吴后，越国大夫范蠡在今中华门外的长干里筑越城，此为南京建城垣之始，距今已近 2470 年。

公元 229 年，三国吴大帝孙权在此建都称建业。都城以今太平路一带为中轴线，南拥秦淮，北枕玄武湖，市井繁富。此后，东晋（公元 317 － 420 年）及南朝（公元 420 － 589 年）的宋、齐、梁、陈均相继在此建都称建康。故南京有"六朝古都"之称。六朝时的建康文化璀璨，商业繁盛，人口多达 140 万左右。由于帝王们崇信佛教，城中的僧尼竟达 10 余万，所造佛寺穷极宏丽，以致唐朝诗人杜牧有"南朝四百八十寺，多少楼台烟雨中"的咏叹。

隋唐之后五代时的中华大地，诸雄相争，战乱不断。而南唐国建都金陵府，偏安江南一隅，境内 70 多年没有发生大的战争。秦淮河两岸集市兴隆、商贾云集。同时，经济繁荣伴随着文化的发达，诗词、书画都开一代之风。

1368 年，明太祖朱元璋（公元 1368 － 1398 年在位）在这里称帝，创建明朝，这里成为华夏的政治中心。他用了21年的时间修建了周长33.65公里的都城城垣，是当时世界上的第一大城。

1853年，太平天国农民革命军攻克南京，在此立都11年，改称天京。1911年爆发的辛亥革命推翻了清王朝的君主统治。同年12月29日，孙中山先生在南京被推选为临时大总统，在这里建立了中华民国。1927年4月18日，蒋介石在南京成立国民政府，南京成了中华民国的首都。

南京城四周山峦起伏，东有最高峰紫金山；北有幕府山峭壁如屏；西有清凉山犹如伏踞之虎，山麓中的清凉寺、扫叶楼一带相传是南唐后主李煜（公元961－975年在位）避暑的地方；城南的雨花台是一座盛产色彩鲜艳玛瑙卵石的山岗；西南有中国佛教的牛头宗发源地牛首山和南唐的先主李昇（公元937－943年在位）和中主李璟（公元943－961年在位）两位皇帝的陵墓所在地祖堂山；城东北的栖霞山，深秋时节，红枫黄槲，层林尽染；临江兀立的燕子矶，山体虽小，但险峻峭拔，宛如欲飞的燕子。

古城既有群山环抱，又有秦淮河、金川河和玄武湖、莫愁湖等大小河流湖泊萦绕、点缀于城中南北。与浩荡的长江一起，组成一曲山川河湖纵横交错的交响诗。难怪三国时，蜀国丞相诸葛亮也不禁赞叹道："钟山龙蟠，石城虎踞，真帝王之宅也。"

南京山环水绕，雄浑深蕴，文化璀璨，名人荟萃，留下众多的名胜古迹。

东郊紫金山麓，吴大帝孙权、明太祖朱元璋以及孙中山先生的陵墓雄伟庄严，浩气磅礴；灵谷寺无梁殿、国民革命军北伐阵亡将士纪念塔、孙中山藏经楼，奇巧无匹；分布在东郊的南朝陵墓石刻放射出中国古代文化的灿烂光芒。

市区的瞻园、煦园是明清两代江南园林艺术的珍品；国内现存最大的中华门城堡和明代城垣以及举世闻名的南京长江大桥更令人留连忘返。

今日的南京是江苏省会，是中国城市综合实力"50强"第五名，是中国东部地区重要的交通和通讯枢纽，是长江三角洲地区仅次于上海的国际性大商埠。

南京市旅游略图
SKETCH TOURIST MAP OF NANJING

长江
Yangtze River

至六合、扬州
To Liuhe, Yangzhou
下关
Xiaguan Road
燕
Xiaguan Road

南京长江大桥
Nanjing Yangtze River Bridge

和燕路
Heyan Road

至上海
To Shanghai

建宁路
Jianning Road

南京西站
West Railway Station

中山码头
Zhongshan Wharf

中山北路
Zhongshan Road North

南京火车站
Nanjing Railway Station

南京饭店
Nanjing Hotel

南京游乐园
Nanjing Amusement Park

江苏展览馆
Jiangsu Exhibition Hall

玄武湖
Xuanwu Lake

鸡鸣寺
Jiming Temple

紫金山天文台
Purple Mountain Observatory

紫金山
Purple Mountain

至栖霞、镇江
To Xixa, Zhenjiang

省政府
Provincial Government

市政府
Municipal Government

中山陵
Sun Yat-sen Mausoleum

灵谷塔
Linggu Pagoda

北京西路
Beijing Road West

北京东路
Beijing Road East

①

④

石头城
Stone City

古南都饭店
Grand Hotel

煦园
Xu Garden

梅园新村纪念馆
Meiyuan Xincun

②

⑥

流徽榭
Liuhui Lakeside Pavilion

四方城
Square City

南京中华织锦村
Nanjing Zhonghua(China)
Brocade Village

莫愁湖公园
Moshou Lake Park

金陵饭店
Jinling Hotel

中山路
Zhongshan Road

中山东路
Zhongshan Road East

南京博物馆
Nanjing Museum

朝天宫
Chaotiangong

金陵刻经处
Jinling Buddhist
Sutras Engraving Studio

明故宫遗址
Ruins of Ming Palace

瞻园
Zhan Garden

夫子庙秦淮风景带
Confucius Temple-Qinhuai
River Scenic Zone

民航售票处
CAAC Nanjing Booking Office

中华门城堡
Zhonghua Gate

秦淮河
Qinhuai River

雨花路
Yuhua Road

雨花台
Rain Flower Terrace

雨花路东
Yuhua Road East

六合
Liuhe

栖霞山风景区
Xixiashan Scenic Area

南京
Nanjing

江宁
Jiangning

阳山碑村
Yangshan
Headstones

句容
Jurong

牛首山
Niushou Hill

鸟鞍山
Ma'anshan

长江
Yangtze River

天生桥
Tiansheng Bridge

① 明孝陵
Xiaoling Mausoleum

② 石象路
Stone Elephant Path

③ 音乐台
Open-air Concert Hall

④ 藏经楼
Classics Depositary

Nanjing

Nanjing is situated in the lower reaches of the Yangtze River, which flows past it from the southwest to the northeast. Here, the river is wide, even the narrowest section exceeding one kilometer in width.

南京

位于长江下游，长江由西南滚滚而来，向东北滔滔而去。这里江面宽阔，最窄处也有1公里多。

Sailing boats on the Yangtze River.

长江风帆

Nanjing Yangtze River Bridge

Designed by China and constructed with home-made materials, this bridge, opened to traffic in October 1968, is a double-decker with a four-lane, 4,589-meter-long highway and 6,772-meter-long double railroad tracks.

南京长江大桥

1968年10月建成通车。是我国自行设计、用自己的材料建造的现代化大桥。公路桥长4589米，铁路桥长6772米。

Mt. Zhongshan As Viewed from a Distance

Also called Purple Mountain, it is 448 meters above sea level and curled like a huge dragon in Nanjing's east suburbs.

远眺钟山

钟山又名紫金山，海拔448米，它像一条巨龙盘亘在南京东郊。

Shitoucheng (Stone City)

Built by Emperor Sun Quan of the Wu Kingdom during the Three Kingdoms Period, it was compared to a "crouching tiger" by the ancients.

石头城

这里古为长江故道，江涛逼城，形势险峻。三国时，吴大帝孙权依山傍江筑石头城，作为军事堡垒。所谓"石城虎踞"指的就是这里。

14

◀ Nanjing City Wall

Extended in the Ming Dynasty on the basis of the Southern Tang wall, it was 33.65 kilometers in girth, 14 to 22 meters in height and 19 meters thick at the base, ranking as the largest city in the world at that time.

南京城垣

是明代在南唐城的基础上扩建而成，周长33.65公里，高14－22米，底部厚19米左右。是当时世界上的第一大城。

Yljiang Gate

An addition to the original 13 gates of Nanjing, then capital of the Ming Dynasty, it was built in the late Qing Dynasty when Nanjing was opened as a foreign trade port and commerce thrived along the banks of the Yangtze.

挹江门

明都城有13门，挹江门不在其列。清末，南京开埠，沿江逐渐繁荣，故开辟海陵门，后改称挹江门。

◀Purple Mountain Observatory

Completed in 1934 after six years of construction, it is the major base of astronomical research in China.

紫金山天文台

于1928年始建，历时6年建成，是我国天文科学研究的主要基地。

Ancient Astronomical Instruments Displayed in Purple Mountain Observatory

These are replicas of the instruments made in 1437 for the Nanjing Imperial Observatory. Originally installed in Beijing, they were plundered by the invaders of the eight-power allied force in 1900 when they overran Beijing. Later the instruments were returned to China and were shipped to Nanjing in 1933.

紫金山天文台陈列的古代天文仪器

是1437年按照南京钦天台的仪器复制安放在北京的。八国联军入侵北京时被掠，后归还中国并于1933年运回南京。

Yangshan Headstones

Chosen originally by the Ming emperor Chengzu for his father's Xiaoling Mausoleum, these stones were too big to be hauled away, so they were left at Yangshan Mountain, where they had been obtained.

阳山碑材

原为明成祖皇帝为其父的孝陵所选的碑材，后因太大，无法运走而弃，至今仍留在江宁阳山。

Square City

So called for its similarity to a citadel, it is a pavilion housing an 8.87-meter-high memorial tablet erected by Chengzu in his father's Xiaoling Mausoleum.

四方城

是孝陵碑亭，碑高8.87米，是明成祖为颂扬其父功德所立。因琉璃瓦亭顶在清代被毁，下半截犹如城垒，故称四方城。

Portrait of Zhu Yuanzhang.
朱元璋画像

The Ming Xiaoling Mausoleum

This tomb of the founding emperor of the Ming Dynasty, Zhu Yuanzhang, is located at the southern foot of the Purple Mountain and is one of the largest imperial tombs in China.

明孝陵

为明朝开国皇帝朱元璋（公元1368－1398年在位）的陵墓，位于紫金山南麓，是我国最大的帝王陵墓之一。

Xiaoling Mausoleum Treasure City

This is actually a grave mound with a diameter of 400 meters, to be reached by a flight of 54 steps.

明孝陵宝城

入拱门，上五十四级台阶，迎面是直径约400米的墓丘。

The Sacred Path to Xiaoling Mausoleum

It is lined on either side with 12 pairs of stone lions, *xiechai* (a fabulous, unicorn-like beast), camels, elephants, *qilin* and horses and four pairs of military and civil officers.

孝陵神道

两侧依次排列着狮、獬豸、骆驼、大象、麒麟、马等石兽6种12对，文臣、武将各两对。神道的规模和石雕个体均是我国古代神道中较大者。

24

Sun Yat-sen Mausoleum

Built with the mountain terrain, this is the tomb of the great revolutionary forerunner, Dr.Sun Yat-sen (1866-1925).

中山陵

是伟大的革命先行者孙中山先生（公元 1866－1925 年）的陵墓。陵墓建筑群巧妙地结合山体形势，庄严而雄伟。

The Memorial Hall in the Sun Yat-sen Mausoleum

In it is a marble seated statue of Dr. Sun Yat-sen and the "Outline for National Construction" in his handwriting carved on the two side walls.

中山陵祭堂

内置孙中山大理石雕坐像，东西两侧护壁上刻有孙中山手书《建国大纲》。

Linggu (Soul Valley) Pagoda

Built in 1930 in memory of the martyrs of the Northern Expeditionery Force of the National Revolutionary Army, the monument is 61 meters in height and 14 meters in diameter at the bottom tier.

灵谷塔

原名国民革命军阵亡将士纪念塔，1930 年为纪念北伐阵亡将士所建。塔高 61 米，底层直径 14 米。

Beamless Hall

Built in 1382 entirely of huge bricks and topped with glazed tiles, it is the earliest and biggest hall of its kind in China.

无梁殿

建于明洪武十四年（公元 1382 年）。整个建筑不用梁柱，全用巨砖垒砌，盖以琉璃瓦，是我国最大、最早的无梁殿宇。

Open-air Concert Hall

Built in 1932, it is located in the southeast of the Sun Yat-sen Mausoleum.

音乐台

在中山陵东南，于 1932 年建成。

Sun Yat-sen Classics Depositary ▶

A palatial, lamasery-like structure built in 1935 to house the classics of Dr. Sun Yat-sen as well as stone carvings.

藏经楼

建于 1935 年，用来收藏孙中山先生经典著作和石刻。是一座中西合璧仿喇嘛寺风格的宫殿建筑。

Zixia (Purple Cloud) Lake

Located east of the Xiaoling Mausoleum. In 1947
Chiang Kai-shek chose a spot here for his future
burial ground.

紫霞湖

在明孝陵东侧。湖畔不远的山腰上建有正气亭，
1947年蒋介石先生曾在此为自己选择日后归葬之
地。

Liuhui Lakeside Pavilion

Built in 1932 In the southeast of the Sun Yat-sen Mausoleum, it stands out in bold relief against a skyline of green trees and hills.

流徽榭

位于中山陵东南，于 1932 年建成。湖面水榭、山林相映，湖畔草坪如茵。

Qinhuai River

A bustling commercial district with a dense population during the Six Dynasties Period and the downtown area in the Ming and Qing dynasties. After much development today it has bacome a tourist attraction and a commercial center with a unique ancient style.

秦淮河

六朝时，这里已是居民密集、商贸繁华的街市。明清两代，这一带更是商肆酒楼林立，亭台楼阁如云。如今经过修整、开发，已成为独具特色的明清风格的游览胜地和商业区。

34

The East Market Located near the Confucius Temple

It is lined with streets modelled after those of the Ming and Qing dynasties, with dozens of shops selling antiques, such as jade objects, traditional stationery and other arts and crafts.

夫子庙东市

夫子庙两侧仿明清街道装修古色古香。这里数十家店铺经营古玩玉器、翰墨文具、工艺制品。

Lantern Festival

It was popularly held in Nanjing as early as in the Six Dynasties Period, lasting for ten nights in the Ming Dynasty. In recent years the Confucius Temple and its vicinity are decorated with a sea of colorful lanterns and people flock there to enjoy the sight every year during the Spring Festival.

灯节

南京在六朝时，灯会就比较兴盛。明朝又将放灯时间延长到十个夜晚，近年春节刚到，夫子庙一带已是彩灯遍地，人山人海了。

Jiangnan Gongyuan

First built in 1169, it became the largest imperial civil examination hall in the Ming-Qing period, with 20,644 rooms for examinees. In recent years some of the rooms have been restored, where such examinations are re-created for interested tourists.

江南贡院

始建于公元1169年，明清两代发展成为全国规模最大的科举考场，仅考生号舍就有20,644间。近年又恢复局部考棚供参观，并组织游客模拟应考。

38

Zhonghua Gate

Known as Jubao (Treasure Accumulation) Gate in the Ming Dynasty, it has three barbicans and four gates. The castle, the largest extant in China, is 128 meters from north to south and 118 meters from east to west, and is capable of stationing 3,000 soldiers.

中华门

即明代的聚宝门，有瓮城三道，门四重。城堡南北长 128 米，东西长 118 米，内有藏兵洞 27 个，可藏甲士 3000，为我国现存最大的城堡。

The jade state seal of the Taiping Heavenly Kingdom.

太平天国玉玺

Zhan (Prospect) Garden

This West Garden of the Prince of Zhongshan, Xu Da, in the Ming Dynasty was the temporary lodging of the Qing Dynasty emperor Qianlong during his inspection tour of South China and later served as the office of the Eastern Prince Yang Xiuqing of the Taiping Heavenly Kingdom.

瞻园

明代为中山王徐达的西花园，清代乾隆皇帝巡游江南曾驻跸这里。太平天国时曾为东王杨秀清衙署。

The Museum of History of the Taiping Heavenly Kingdom in the Zhan Garden.

瞻园内的太平天国历史博物馆

◀ Rain Flower Terrace Cemetery for Fallen Heroes

Built in 1950 in memory of the revolutionary martyrs killed by the Kuomintang government.

雨花台烈士陵园

1950年为纪念被国民党政府屠杀的革命烈士而建。

Rain Flower Terrace Pebbles

These colorful stones, for which the Rain Flower Terrace is known, are "worth a hundred taels of gold" as an ancient saying goes.

雨花石

雨花台盛产玛瑙石、色彩绚丽、玲珑剔透，尤以花纹奇巧者为精品，自古即有百金易一石的记载。

Nanjing Yun (Cloud) Brocade

One of China's three famous brocades, it was used exclusively by the imperial houses or as gifts bestowed by the emperors on princes or senior officials. Today it is still woven by hand with traditional knowhow.

南京云锦

为中国传统三大名锦之一。过去专供宫廷御用和赏赐王公大臣之用，至今仍采用特殊传统手工工艺编织。

Jinling Buddhist Sutras Engraving Studio

A world-renowned institution specializing in editing, engraving and printing Buddhist classics set up by lay Buddhist Yang Renshan in 1866.

金陵刻经处

是国内外享有盛名的近代编校刻印佛典的专门机构。由杨仁山居士于 1866 年始创。

◀ Mochou (Don't Worry) Lake

Formed of an old channel of the Yangtze in the 10th century, it is named after a pretty, hard-working girl once living by the lake.

莫愁湖

位于城西。原为长江故道，约于10世纪时形成湖泊，因湖畔曾住过一位勤劳美丽的少女莫愁而得名。

Shengqi (Victory at Chess) Pavilion

A gift bestowed by the Ming emperor Zhu Yuanzhang on his defense minister Xu Da after a merry chess game.

莫愁湖胜棋楼

相传明太祖朱元璋曾在此与徐达对弈，徐达在围棋盘上下出了"万岁"二字，太祖高兴，将楼赐予徐达。

Xuanwu Lake

Surrounded by hills on three sides and the city wall on one side, it was a pleasure ground of the emperors and a training center for imperial navies during the Six Dynasties Period (420-589), but was turned into a park in the late Qing Dynasty.

玄武湖

六朝时即为帝王们游乐和训练水军的地方，清朝末年辟为公园。公园总面积 444 公顷，湖面三面环山一面临城。

Xuanzhuang Stupa on Mt.Jiuhua

In 1943, when the Japanese invaders in Nanjing discovered the skull cap of the famous Tang Dynasty monk Xuanzhuang at the former site of the Greater Bao'en Temple, they sent part of it to Japan and kept the remainder in the stupa they built.

九华山玄奘塔

1943年侵华日军在南京大报恩寺旧址掘得唐代高僧玄奘顶骨，部分运往日本。剩余部分归瘗现址并造塔建殿。

50

Jiming (Cockcrow) Temple

First built in the Ming Dynasty and rebuilt in 1981, with a 44-meter-high pagoda, it used to be a rendezvous of scholars in the Six Dynasties Period.

鸡鸣寺

六朝时这里是文士聚集的儒馆，明代在这里建鸡鸣寺，后屡毁屡建。1981年又重建。寺塔高44米。

Chaotiangong (Hall of Tribute to the Son of Heaven)

Said to be the former site of the "metallurgical city" erected by Prince Fu Chai of Wu. The only building now extant there is the Confucius Temple built in the reign of Emperor Tongzhi (1862-1874).

朝天宫

相传为吴王夫差所筑冶城故址，明代建为演习朝贺天子礼仪的朝天宫，现存建筑为清同治年间（公元 1862 – 1874 年）重建的文庙。

◀ Catholic Cathedral on Shigu Road

This Gothic-style structure was built by a French missionary in 1870. Another cathedral, built earlier by the Italian missionary Matteo Ricci, had fallen into ruin.

石鼓路天主教堂

意大利传教士利玛窦传教时曾建造教堂，后毁。1870 年由法籍教士在今址修建了这组"哥特式"天主教堂。

Nanjing Massacre Memorial Hall

Erected in 1985 in memory of the 300,000 fellow countrymen murdered by the Japanese invaders in 1937.

侵华日军南京大屠杀遇难同胞纪念馆

1985 年，为纪念 1937 年日军侵占南京屠城时死难的 300,000 同胞而建，位于城西江东门。

53

◀ Xu (Radiance) Garden

Originally the west garden of the Mansion of the Heavenly King of the Taiping Heavenly Kingdom and later of the Presidential Palace of the Republic of China, it is the gem of southern garden art of the Ming and Qing dynasties.

煦园

原为太平天国天王府及民国总统府内的西侧花园，故又称西花园，是明清两代江南园林艺术的结晶。

Stone Boat in Radiance Garden

Here Taiping generals sometimes met to discuss important military matters and Dr.Sun Yat-sen often received his guests.

不系舟

西花园内的石舫，因清乾隆皇帝题额而得名。太平天国将领曾在此商讨军机大事。孙中山亦常在此接待宾客。

56

Provisional President Sun Yat-sen's Office

Formerly the parlor of the Liangjiang viceroy's mansion in the Qing Dynasty, where Dr. Sun assumed office as Provisional President of the Republic of China in 1912.

孙中山临时大总统办公室

原为清朝两江总督所造的花厅。1912年元旦，孙中山于此就任中华民国临时大总统。

57

The Presidential Palace

Formerly the Liangjiang viceroy's mansion and the mansion of the Heavenly King of the Taiping Heavenly Kingdom, it became the residence of the President of the National Government in 1927.

总统府

原为清朝的两江总督府，太平天国时为天王府，后为中华民国临时政府，1927 年改建为国民政府的总统府。

Nanjing Museum

Built in 1933 at the celebrated educationist Cai Yuanpei's proposal and renamed National Nanjing Museum in 1950, it is home to 420,000 historical relics.

南京博物院

1933年由著名教育家蔡元培（公元1868–1940年）倡议筹建。1950年命名为国立南京博物院。内收藏历代文物珍品42万余件。

Silver-inlaid Bronze Ox Lamp

Made in the Eastern Han Dynasty (25-220), this 46.2-cm-high treasure has a beautiful contour.

错银铜牛灯

东汉（公元 25－220 年）时制，灯高 46.2cm。
造型优美，堪为珍品。灯燃时烟炱可通过粗管，
经牛头吸入牛腹。

Stone Carvings in Southern Dynasties Tombs

Scattered in 20 spots around Nanjing, these gems of the Six Dynasties culture include this *qilin* (unicorn) guarding the Sacred Path that leads to the Yongning Tomb of the Chen Dynasty emperor Wendi (r.560-566).

南朝陵墓石刻

分布于南京周围，约 20 处，为我国六朝文化艺术的珍品。图为陈文帝（公元 560 – 566 年在位）永宁陵神道麒麟。

The *pixie* Mythical Beast in Front of Xiao Dan's Tomb of the Liang Dynasty

The stone beasts guarding the Sacred Path to Six Dynasties emperors' tombs are *qilin* and *tianlu* while those guarding the tombs of princes and senior ministers are *pixie*.

梁代萧憺墓前辟邪

六朝时期皇帝陵前的神道石兽为麒麟和天禄，而王公大臣神道石兽为辟邪。

Stone *pixie* on the Sacred Path to Xiao Jing's tomb, Liang Dynasty.

梁代萧景墓神道石刻辟邪

Xixia (Cloud Nestling) Temple ▶

This temple, located 20 km northeast of Nanjing and famous for its stupas and cliff sculptures, dates back to the Six Dynasties Period.

栖霞寺

位于城东北二十公里的栖霞山凤翔峰下，是著名的六朝古刹，有舍利塔、千佛岩摩崖石刻等珍贵遗迹。

◀ Cloud Nestling Temple Stupa

First built in the Sui Dynasty (581-618) and rebuilt in the Southern Tang period.

栖霞寺舍利塔

始建于隋朝（公元581－618年），南唐时重修。

Tiansheng Bridge

This 34-meter-long structure, 35 meters above the Yanzhi Canal, was dug out of a cliff early in the Ming Dynasty for the purpose of transporting southern grain to the national capital.

天生桥

明初，朱元璋为漕运南方粮赋进都城，开凿胭脂河时，利用天然石岗凿成桥梁。桥长34米，离水面高达35米。

Two Southern Tang Mausoleums

The tombs of the first two Southern Tang emperors, Li Bian and Li Jing, where more than 600 cultural relics were brought to light in 1950.

南唐二陵

五代南唐先主李昇和中主李璟两个皇帝的陵墓，1950年发现，地宫早被盗过，但仍出土600多件珍贵文物。

Hongjue (Broad Awakening) Temple Pagoda

Built in 774 on the pine-covered Ox Head Hill in the south suburbs, this tourist attraction is known for its picturesque scenery.

牛首山宏觉寺塔

建于唐大历9年（公元774年）。南郊的牛首山自古松竹掩映，寺庙众多。阳春三月，更是山花烂漫，风景如画。

Children playing on a platform at the Ming imperial palace site.

在明故宫遗址石础上玩耍的孩童

Making steamed glutinous rice cakes.

蒸儿糕

Moulding dough **figurines.**

捏面人

Summer in Nanjing

The municipal government has paid close attention to greening the city, one of the "four big ovens" in China. Afforestation in recent years has resulted in a drop of the mean summer temperature in Nanjing.

南京之夏

南京夏季炎热，是中国四大"火炉"之一，由于多年来注意城市绿化，夏季平均温度略有下降。

A Nanjing boulevard.
南京林荫大道

图书在版编目（CIP）数据

南京：英汉对照／兰佩瑾编；刘晓梵文。－北京：外文出版社，1997
ISBN 7-119-01970-8

I.南… II.①兰…②刘… III.南京－摄影集 IV.J426.531
中国版本图书馆CIP数据核字（96）第 22144 号

Edited by: Lan Peijin
Text by: Liu Xiaofan
Photos by: Liu Xiaofan   Lan Peijin   Guo Qun
He Zhaoxin   Liu Dajian   Ru Xuan
Wang Chengyou
Translated by: Fang Zhiyun
Bookcover designed by: Tang Shaowen
Plates designed by: Cai Rong   Zhou Tongyu

编辑：兰佩瑾
撰文：刘晓梵
摄影：刘晓梵   兰佩瑾   郭　群
何兆欣   刘大健   王承友
汝　萱
翻译：方芷筠
封面设计：唐少文
图版设计：蔡　荣   周彤宇

南　京

兰佩瑾 编

＊

ⓒ 外文出版社

外文出版社出版
（中国北京百万庄大街24号）
邮政编码 100037
捷诚印务(深圳)有限公司印刷
1997 年（24开）第一版
1997 年第一版第一次印刷

Nanjing

ISBN 7-119-01970-8

ⓒ Foreign Languages Press

Published by Foreign Languages Press
24 Baiwanzhuang Road, Beijing 100037, China
Printed in the People's Republic of China

ISBN 7--0-8 /J·1395